RENOIR

Renoir

by Bruno F. Schneider

CROWN TRADE PAPERBACKS - NEW YORK

Title page: SELF-PORTRAIT, 1876
Oil on canvas, 29″ × 22½″ (73.7 × 60.1 cm)
The Fogg Art Museum, Cambridge, Massachusetts
Bequest Collection Maurice Wertheim

Series published under the direction of:
MADELEINE LEDIVELEC-GLOECKNER

Translated by:
DESMOND AND CAMILLE CLAYTON

Published by Crown Trade Paperbacks,
201 East 50th Street, New York, New York 10022.
Member of the Crown Publishing Group.

Random House, Inc. New York, Toronto, London, Sydney, Auckland

CROWN TRADE PAPERBACKS and colophon are trademarks of Crown Publishers, Inc.
Originally published in hardcover by Crown Publishers, Inc., in 1977.

Printed in Italy – Poligrafiche Bolis S.P.A., Bergamo

Library of Congress Cataloging-in-Publication Data

Schneider, Bruno F.
Renoir.
(Crown art library)
Bibliography: p. 93
1. Renoir, Auguste, 1841–1919. 2. Painting, French.
3. Painting, Modern—19th century—France. 4. Painting,
Modern—20th century—France. 5. Impressionism (Art)—
France. I Title. II. Series.
ND553.R45A4 1987   759.4   87-22356

ISBN 0-517-88415-1

10 9 8 7 6 5 4 3 2 1

First Paperback Edition

THE SEINE AT ARGENTEUIL, 1873. Oil on canvas, 19¾″ × 25¾″ (50.2 × 65.5 cm)
Portland Art Museum, Oregon. Bequest of Winslow B. Ayer

«Like a child, I paint before nature with an artless soul and the instincts of my fingertips.»

PIERRE-AUGUSTE RENOIR

If such words were to be spoken in the latter part of the 20th century they would sound, in relation to the the aims of our artists, be they objective or abstract, immodest, incredibly arrogant, for the words «an artless soul and the instincts of the fingertips» describe in simple terms the highest ideals of the painting of today, ideals, moreover, which are seldom attained. Renoir, however, did attain them. And yet these words were not the outcome of an artist's

Edmond Renoir at Menton, 1883
Ink and crayon. Private collection

pride, but of a great and gentle modesty, a humbleness before the creation and its creatures, and before art. These words do not imply « I have achieved, » but « I was allowed to achieve. » Renoir was, after all, not an intellectual artist who strove to vitalize his work by means of reflected naïveté, but a man who presented the world afresh, consonant with himself, his soul, and his ability. One hesitates to apply the word « genius » to him, because this word does not necessarily imply the fecundity and simplicity which was Renoir's and which made his pictures resemble happy natural phenomena. There is no doubt, however, that he was a genius if one takes genius to comprise the powers of a pure and vital soul, and an inexhaustible creative urge. Renoir said of himself once, half regretfully and half proudly: « I am like a small cork which has fallen into the water and is being carried away by the current. I surrender myself unconditionally to painting. » His genius consisted in the inexhaustibility of his visions which gently, but irresistibly, demanded expression. All the rest was craftsmanship: Sterling craftsmanship and iron assiduity, for Renoir began as a craftsman, as a porcelain painter, and took the path of diligence to great art and fulfilment.

It is high time for the word color to be mentioned, for to speak of Renoir is to speak of color. It is true, of course, that all the Impressionists worshipped color and light. In Renoir's pictures, however, they develop into ecstatic feasts, the light takes on material qualities, it foams and sparkles in his pictures, and sometimes illuminates the colors like precious stones. If one of his works were taken into a gallery of pictures by the official masters of the Ecole des Beaux-Arts of the 19th century, all the rest would dissolve into a dirty blackish brown, compared with Renoir's brilliant colors. Even the pictures by moderate revolutionaries, like those of Corot, with their silvery twilight, or of Daubigny, with their delicate, lustrous colors, fade into darkness before an early Renoir like *Lise* in the Folkwang Museum in Essen. And this despite the fact that in this picture he still has both feet planted firmly on the ground of tradition, and that color was only to reach its full maturity in his later pictures, in which it seems to have become luminescent. There are no longer reflections of sunlight, which, in the early garden pictures, for example, were applied with thick strokes of the brush. Now the paint has thinned, and the canvas appears to be transilluminated from behind. This paradise of color, which surpasses all Impressionist theories, is Renoir's great gift to the world.

The lives of the French Impressionists, Renoir's older and younger contemporaries, lend themselves all too easily to romantic biography. Names like Manet, Pissarro, Monet, and Sisley conjure up the Paris of artists and literati described by Henry Murger in his famous «Scenes of Bohemian Life,» the Paris of small cafés and bars, of countless art dealers and booksellers, the Paris of attic studios surrounded by a forest of black chinney pots with their creaking cowls. All the misery and ecstasy, all the poverty and glory of the artist's life was realized in the lives of that generation of painters. They sounded all the material and intellectual heights and depths, and took possession of the world with tremendous vitality; their world was the present. In a passionate reaction against the now impotent historicity of 19th century art the Impressionists took a decisive step towards the problems of the day. Historical themes and historical costumes disappeared from their pictures, and the obligatory pilgrimages of artists to the home of antique art were a thing of the past.

Couple on a Slope, 1883
Pencil. Private collection

The watchword was contemporaneousness — «être de son temps» — in the true sense of the word. The only things worthy of representation in painting are those things that happen, and are seen, today. That is the spirit of Impressionism. This assertion allowed of variation: One group — Boudin, Pissarro, Sisley — concerned themselves with landscape as being absolutely unhistorical and always modern; others, like Degas, studied the physiognomy and gestures of the people of their time and tried to create valid symbols for them. Manet invented a new style, flat, unceremonious, loud, which consciously contrasted with the dignified representation of important events in the painting of the past. Modernness was the passion, «contemporanéité» was the rational ground for existence. One lived in Paris without being established there, was social without social ambitions, enjoyed the moment today, without granting it a sentimental thought tomorrow. Only a few could resist the attraction of this way of life. Cézanne, for example, whose modest income enabled him to lead an outwardly calm bourgeois existence. Renoir, however, who had decided to take up painting in Paris at the age of twenty-one although he was without any real means, would have been just the type for the Bohemian life of Paris if his character and origin had not endowed him with powers to protect him from unconditional fanatical concentration on the present. In order to understand those powers, it is necessary to go back to his earliest youth, even to his birth.

It is very tempting to place significance on the fact that it happened to be the town of Limoges where Pierre-Auguste Renoir was born on February 25, 1841: The town where, toward the end of the 15th century, art enamel was first produced and handed down from father to son in several artists' families till the end of the 17th century. It really seems as if the spirit of one of the great Limoges enamel painters had instilled into the child his love of bright, shining colors, his delicate taste, and his feeling for craftsmanship. But it was not only a case of the influence of the genius loci, for Renoir gained a thorough knowledge in the use of colors, and above all a love of good and lasting craftsmanship in five years of work in a Paris workshop for porcelain painting. The boy had to start work at the age of ten, as his father, a modest tailor from Limoges, had moved with his family to Paris in the vain hope of finding a better living there. Pierre-Auguste had to help to support the family, and the beginning in the porcelain workshop was very promising. The work gave him a light touch and a sure eye for the selection and combination of colors. Soon he had progressed from decorative to figurative work, and his repertoire ran from floral patterns to the portrait of Marie-Antoinette, for which he was paid forty centimes apiece. The colors with which he mainly worked were those of the rococo period: delicate pinks, brilliant blues, and chrome yellow, on the gleaming white kaolin background. This trio of colors occurs again and again in his later pictures, where they are supplemented by many shades of green, violet, and a brilliant, fatty black. Those five years were happy ones for him, but came to an end through the invention of a system of printing on porcelain, which ousted the craftsman in favor of a mechanical process. Renoir joined the workshop of a fan painter; here he painted scenes of gallantry after Boucher, Watteau, and Lancret. Later he painted screens and decorations for mobile mission altars. The young journeyman was soon superior to his fellow-workers and the master, and was called a «baby Rubens» because of the astonishing bravura with which he handled color.

His later development into a great artist, however, was decisively influenced by his early range of motifs as well as by his foundation of craftsmanship. Rococo pastoral scenes like *Embarkation to Cythera* by Watteau were always in demand, and Renoir had to provide them. So he spent his little free time in the Louvre where he diligently studied the composition of the French painters of the 18th century, their colors and their virtuoso brush technique. He fell in love with the spirit of that period, and its elegance and lightness inspired his brush. It permeates his later works, despite the manifold influences of Courbet, Delacroix, and Ingres, like a tender melody, only occasionally obscured by the noises of the present.

Although his work for the missions promised to be very successful financially, and would have guaranteed him a modest career as an arts and crafts worker, he gave notice to his employer. He had saved enough money to be able to attend painting and drawing courses at the Ecole des Beaux-Arts. At the same time he joined Gleyre's studio. As with most of the teachers who had their own schools, Gleyre's connection with the Ecole, the stronghold of the austere academic art, was very vague, and he was known among students of painting for his generosity and his artistic tolerance. Himself only a mediocre historical painter, his greatest importance lies in the fact that he taught the young generation the fundamental technical craftsmanship of painting without forcing their talent to conform to the Procrustes bed of traditional style. Renoir and his thirty or forty fellow students drew diligently from

THE SWING, 1876. Oil on canvas, 35⅜″ × 30″ (92 × 73 cm)
Musée du Louvre, Jeu de Paume, Paris

THE LOGE, 1874. Oil on canvas, 32″ × 25″ (80 × 64 cm)
Courtauld Institute Galleries, London. The Courtauld Collection

THE FIRST EVENING OUT, 1876. Oil on canvas, 25½″ × 19⅝″ (65 × 50 cm)
The National Gallery, London

PENSIVE, c. 1875. Oil on canvas, $18\frac{1}{8}'' \times 15''$ (46 × 38.1 cm)
Virginia Museum of Fine Arts, Richmond, Virginia. Collection of Mr. and Mrs. Paul Mellon

GEORGES RIVIÈRE, 1877. Oil on canvas, 14½″ × 11½″ (36.8 × 29.3 cm)
National Gallery of Art, Washington D.C. Collection Ailsa Mellon Bruce

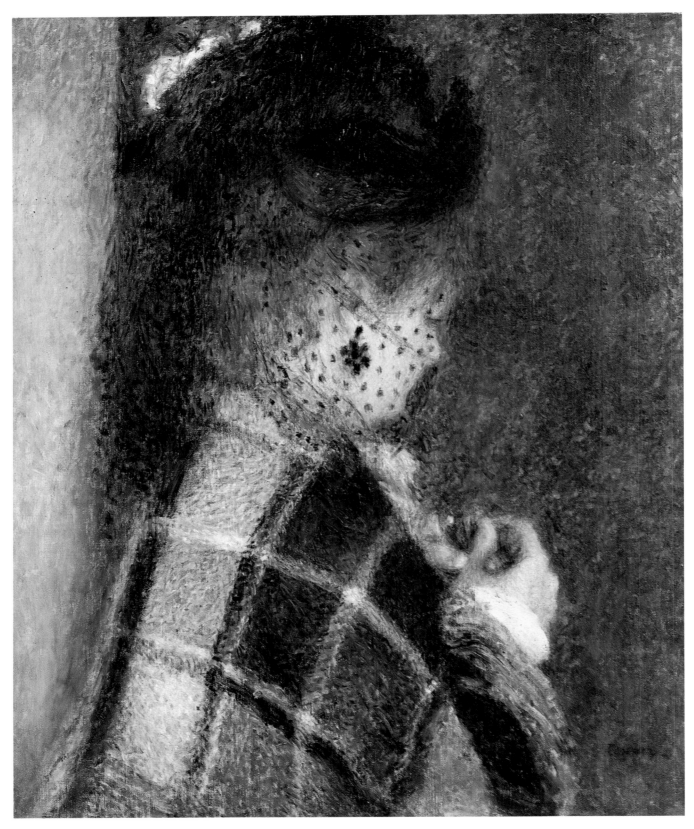

LADY WITH VEIL, c. 1875. Oil on canvas, 24″ × 20″ (61 × 51 cm)
Musée du Louvre, Jeu de Paume, Paris

THÉRÈSE BÉRARD, 1879. Oil on canvas, 22″ × 18⁷⁄₁₆″ (55.9 × 46.8 cm)
Sterling and Francine Clark Art Institute, Williamstown, Massachusetts

THE UMBRELLAS
1883
Oil on canvas
71″ × 59″
(190 × 115 cm)
The National
Gallery, London

the nude at Gleyre's. One week the model was male, the next female. Twice a week Gleyre went to the studio and corrected the perspective, the anatomy, the plastic effect of the body, and the color. It was on such an occasion, when he was standing, no doubt a little nonplussed, in front of one of Renoir's daringly colored pictures, that he disapprovingly asked if the pupil was painting for enjoyment. When Renoir innocently answered in the affirmative—«if I didn't enjoy it I shouldn't do it»—Gleyre was not a little astonished, because nobody had ever yet painted there for fun. However boisterous and Bohemian the activities may have been in all the painting classes of the Ecole while the teacher's back was turned, painting was a deadly serious thing for the young artists. They saw their careers in their various stages stretching out quite clearcut in front of them. The annual exams, competition for the «Prix de Rome,» the scholarships, the acceptance of their pictures for the annual Salon d'Automne, and finally the commissioning of works by the state. In the distance beckoned the honor

Young Girl with Rose, 1886
Pastel. Private collection, Paris

of being made «Chevalier de la Légion d'Honneur» and a member of the Academy. But Renoir painted because he enjoyed it.

There was also one other student who was a source of considerable difficulty for Gleyre. It was Monet, who, in Le Havre, where he had spent his youth, had already achieved some success as a caricaturist. Gleyre disapproved of his pictures, too, because the young man reproduced the models with merciless accuracy just as they were—with too large feet, with a short, thickset body, or with a thick skull. Gleyre criticized him and instructed him to reproduce the model in an idealized form according to the then valid classical canons of beauty. If in Renoir's daring use of color the dangerous influence of Delacroix was suspected, the Delacroix who was already poisoning the youngest students and alienating them from the principle that the line was the only valid medium of artistic expression, in Monet the academicians saw the realism of Courbet, who must have appeared to them to be no less corrupting. The corrections made by these teachers of the Ecole were like somebody hastily papering over the cracks in the wall of a house in the hope of thus saving the whole structure from ruin while decay was already taking its irresistible course in the foundations.

There were in fact signs of crisis in the Ecole des Beaux-Arts and the whole of its official art. Everybody felt it, supporters and enemies. Renoir and Monet quickly became known among the Gleyre students as revolutionaries, although they, unlike the others, sat quietly and diligently behind their easels: At that time it was considered much more reprehensible to apply a certain burning red to the canvas than, for example, to throw dripping paint brushes at the model when the teacher was absent. The beginning of the crisis in academic painting, glaringly obvious by the time Renoir, Monet, Bazille, and Sisley were attending Gleyre's studio and the Ecole, can be traced back to the year 1855, when a comprehensive international art exhibition, in which the French section took up most space, was assembled in Paris for the great World's Fair. At that time Courbet already dared to rebel against the artistic dictatorship of the all-powerful director of the Académie des Beaux-Arts, Count Nieuwekerke, and he opened an exhibition of his rejected pictures near the exhibition building. His « Pavillon du Réalisme » was the opening shot in the battle. Delacroix was driven into the opposition's camp at the same time, for, although a large number of his pictures were exhibited, the majority of the medals and prizes went to Ingres and his supporters. Thus the artists were split into two camps, which fought one another with brush and pen, in the press and in public meetings, with intrigues and physical force. The battle cries were « Hurrah for classical idealism, » « Hurrah for realism, » « Hurrah for line, » « Hurrah for color. » Ingres, the members of the Académie and the teachers of the Ecole stood on the one side, Delacroix, Courbet, and the painters of the Barbizon school on the other. An unequal battle, if one considers the outward positions of power. Behind Ingres stood the Académie des Beaux-Arts, as one of the departments of the Institut de France: The patron, but also the absolute ruler of the arts and sciences. The influence of the Académie extended to the Ecole des Beaux-Arts whose teachers were elected by it. Moreover, the juries in charge of admission of works to the exhibitions and the distributions of prizes were under its authority. Finally the Académie had the decisive word concerning purchases by museums and the official commissioning of artists. As the public accepted the judgment of the institution without reservation an artist outlawed by the Académie was as good as non-existent; he had no chance of even exhibiting his works.

Renoir and his friends at Gleyre's took no part in these battles or in the preparations for the Salon d'Automne in 1862. They themselves could not yet think of submitting anything for the exhibition but they watched the hectic activity of their older colleagues: Press opinion was bought, individual members of the jury were waited on, the hanging committee was bribed so that the pictures which were finally accepted were also advantageously placed. The business of art devoured everyone's energy, and social reputation was more important than artistic quality. A further symptom of the decrepitude of the official art institutions was the sudden influx of students to the studio of the heretic Courbet, where models were painted realistically. The academic training bored the art students, and so they sought for new stimuli. On the other hand the jury applied even stricter standards for the current exhibition than before — after they had first protected themselves against blunders by abandoning the system of anonymous entry. It could no longer happen that anonymous works by the most important members of the Académie were rejected. That was the situation before the Salon d'Automne of 1863, which was the immediate cause of the outbreak of the battle. This time Renoir had also submitted a picture, a female nude reclining on a divan, with a dwarf next to her

Young Girl. Collection Albertina, Vienna

playing a guitar—an absolutely academic motif, painted, as far as one can judge from contemporary reports, in dark academic colors.

When it became known that the jury had this time rejected more than four thousand works, there was a revolt of the painters who had had their works rejected. Many of them had been represented in previous exhibitions. Among them were Jongkind and Manet, who, with his *Spanish Guitarist*, had already enjoyed great success. Renoir's picture was of course also rejected. The general indignation came to the ears of Emperor Napoleon III, and since, for reasons of prestige, he could no longer cancel the decision of the official jury, he gave the sensational order for the establishment of the Salon des Refusés, which gave every artist the chance of exhibiting or withdrawing his rejected works. Many wisely withdrew so as to avoid the jury's anger on later occasions. The avant-garde, including Whistler, Fantin-Latour, Pissarro, and Cézanne, exhibited, of course. Perhaps the artists had hoped that the public would declare for them, and that the jury would have to be dismissed. In that, however, they had deceived themselves, for the masses demanded their heroic scenes and their genre pictures, meticulously painted, and their still lifes with naturalistic apples to make their mouths water, and noble nude studies of similar effect. For example, a leg in the foreground would have to be executed down to the smallest detail, contours were not allowed to swim, and objects in the background had to appear darker. The public made fun of the Salon des Refusés, while the press split into two camps. Zola discovered an intellectual affinity with this opposition, this revolutionary spirit, and he greeted the exhibition and its artists with enthusiasm, many of whom were, after all, his friends. The critic and writer Zacharie Astruc took a similar attitude. The official art critics, on the other hand, spewed hatred and irony. It is true that the public was amused by the battles, but at least its attention was drawn to the abuses in the art world; the Académie finally found itself forced radically to reorganize itself. But it was too late. The students changed to other schools, and above all the Louvre was filled with copyists who believed that they could learn more from the old masters than from the traditional school. Gleyre's studio was also deserted, and closed in 1864. Thus the friends Renoir, Monet, Bazille, and Sisley were thrown upon their own resources.

Now Monet, who was older and more experienced than the others, became the driving force. He had once before painted on the French Atlantic coast near Le Havre with Boudin and Jongkind. After the Gleyre studio shut down he set up his easel once more in the open air. He took his friends with him, and painted in the forest of Fontainebleau near Chailly. The industrious Renoir, who was always so ready to learn, by no means approved of the turn things had taken because he had enjoyed studying at Gleyre's. He could not know that a meeting of decisive importance for him would take place in the forest of Fontainebleau. Diaz, who belonged to the group of painters who had settled in nearby Barbizon and changed from historical scenes to landscapes, watched Renoir at work and criticized his frequent use of dark colors. He instructed Renoir in the constant and exact observation of nature and opened his eyes to the endless variety of nuances and shades of color which could be found, for example, on the ground in a wood. This meeting spelled Renoir's liberation from those dark tones which gave the works of all the academic painters of that period the appearance of old, smoke darkened antiques.

Nevertheless Renoir's generation's most important discoveries lay not so much in the realm of color as in that of content. In this field Courbet was still the ideal. Renoir emulated him, and painted works even in his later years that recall the blunt realism of that artist; and as long as he took over Courbet's subjects he used Courbet's dark tones. Another ideal was the notorious Manet, who had dared taking up in his picture *The Picnic*, an idea from one of Giorgione's pictures, to show a nude woman next to two men in modern, fashionable clothes. What was permitted for an Italian at the turn of the 15ᵗʰ century was considered indecent in Manet. Thus Renoir also painted a realistic picture in which he depicted his friends in the Cabaret de la Mère Anthony, smoking and chatting, with the pretty and reputedly wanton owner's daughter clearing the table, and, between scribblings on a wall in the background, a charcoal caricature of Murger. This harmless genre piece, already painted, by the way, with an enchanting softness and with a strong plastic quality, was nevertheless far removed from

Manet's vigorous and audacious actuality. On another occasion Renoir tried to emulate Courbet's technique, in that he applied his paint with a knife instead of with a brush. The surface of a woodland scene near Fontainebleau with his friend Lecœur thus took on a coarse structure, as though thick oil paint had been applied to rough masonry. This technique, however, was not consistent with his artistic ideals, which were already calling for a more delicate and subtle use of color. But he continued to experiment, although every now and again, since he found it difficult to burn his boats as uncompromisingly as Monet did for example, he would produce a picture completely academic in content and form. No doubt Renoir kept one eye on the Salon, and his pictures in the academic manner may have been painted with a view to securing an acceptance for the Salon d'Automne. It is a fact that his *Esmeralda*, painted in the academic style, depicting the beautiful gipsy woman of Victor Hugo's «Notre-Dame de Paris» dancing in the Place de Grève, was accepted in 1864. But this success did not give him undiluted pleasure. It may even have seemed to him somewhat dishonest, for although he had not become a fanatical follower of plein-airism — painting in the open air in natural light — the dark «academic sauce» had been distasteful to him ever since his meeting with Diaz. Therefore he destroyed the picture soon afterwards. In 1865, however, two pictures, which remembering Diaz's advice he had painted directly from nature, were accepted.

His period of experimentation lasted until the outbreak of war in 1870. But that period produced two famous works which were important to his artistic development. One of them is the *Lise with Parasol* (1867). Here, for the first time, he carries his idea of colored shadows to its logical conclusion. The delicate, blossom-white dress of the girl is painted with infinite love, weightless, it seems not to have been applied with the brush but to have been breathed on to the canvas. Blue and violet shadows play on it and on the white hat there are reflections from the green foliage. Renoir's brush technique is in the tradition of the old masters. The colors are carefully and smoothly applied, so that there are no individual brush strokes to be seen.

Only two years later, however, in the picture *La Grenouillère*, Renoir managed to free himself completely of the past also in the technical sense: The picture shows a few boats on the water, a colorful gathering on a small island, and a wooded bank in the background. To give the spectator an impression of the reflections dancing on the wavelets, reflections which here have formed a bizarre image of the people and things on the bank, and there have been dispersed by a breath of wind into small patches of dark and light, Renoir uses clearly defined brush strokes. If one placed any value on dating a phenomenon of painting technique — in this case the brush stroke characteristic of Impressionism — one could do it here, for in this picture of Renoir's, and in that of his friend Monet, who painted the same subject at the same time, appear for the first time small patches of color, which, at a certain distance, give the spectator the complex impression of a blue-green pattern of wavelets.

Such discoveries were always sensational for the young painters, who passed paintings around among themselves, and vigorously discussed quality and technique. Before the Franco-Prussian War, which interrupted work and social life for a time, the meeting place

22

Madame Charpentier and Her Children, 1878
Oil on canvas, 60½″ × 74⅛″ (153.7 × 190.2 cm)
The Metropolitan Museum of Art, New York
Catharine Lorillard Wolfe Collection

Claude Renoir, 1904. Lithograph

was either near Paris on the Grenouillère («frog pond») in Père Fournaises's restaurant in Bougival, which had become Monet's and Renoir's haunt, or in Paris itself in the Quartier Batignolles. Here the Café Guerbois was the Impressionists' meeting place. Apart from Renoir, Monet, Sisley, and Bazille, Manet also occasionally put in an appearance. Although

WOMAN WITH A PARASOL AND A SMALL CHILD ON A SUNLIT HILLSIDE, 1877
Oil on canvas, 18½″ × 22⅛″ (47 × 56.2)
Museum of Fine Arts, Boston, Massachusetts. Bequest of John T. Spaulding

LADY AT THE PIANO, 1875. Oil on canvas, 36⅝″ × 29½″ (93 × 75 cm)
The Art Institute of Chicago. Mr. and Mrs. Martin A. Ryerson Collection

MADAME HENRIOT, c. 1876. Oil on canvas, 26″ × 19⅝″ (65.9 × 49.8 cm)
National Gallery of Art, Washington D.C. Gift of the Adele R. Levy Fund

Portrait of Victor Chocquet, 1876. Oil on canvas, 18⅛″ × 14⅛″ (46 × 36 cm)
The Oskar Reinhart Collection «Am Römerholz,» Winterthur, Switzerland

PORTRAIT OF JEANNE SAMARY, 1877. Oil on canvas, $18\frac{1}{8}'' \times 15\frac{3}{4}''$ (46×40 cm)
Comédie Française, Paris

VENICE, THE DOGE'S PALACE, 1881
Oil on canvas, 21 3/8″ × 25 11/16″ (54.3 × 65.3 cm)
Sterling and Francine Clark Art Institute, Williamstown, Massachusetts

SAN MARCO, VENICE, 1881
Oil on canvas, 25¾″ × 32″ (65.5 × 81.3 cm)
The Minneapolis Institute of Arts. The John R. Van Derlip Fund

he did not like to «fraternize» with the Bohemians because he had hopes of one day being recognized by the Académie, he nevertheless felt very much at home in that circle of kindred spirits. Pissarro and Cézanne, and the caustic, intellectual Degas also belonged to the circle.

Renoir himself felt completely at home among this group of friends. He laughed at the jokes though he was often bored by the heated arguments, for nothing was more foreign to him than theoretical discussions on art. He believed in experiment, not theory. Any kind of fanatical devotion to a particular idea, style, or technique, was also foreign to his nature. Even though he was dubbed a revolutionary at the Ecole, he was an «unwilling» revolutionary. He certainly did not want to rouse the world, or bring new truths to light: he quite simply wanted to give pleasure with his pictures. To startle conventional people was not in tune with his optimistic, philanthropic being. A feeling for the relationship between artist and public had remained more vital in him than in any other Impressionist, indeed, perhaps he was the only one in whom it survived at all. That was something he had learned in his youth when he had had to work to order as a craftsman in direct contact with the customer. Art for art's sake has no place in craftsmanship, and as Renoir painted his pictures with the same joy of creation as he had decorated his porcelain, fans, and screens, art for art's sake had no place in his painting either. For Renoir, then, it was not a question of conscience whether one should make compromises or not in order to get a picture into an exhibition. For him it was at most a question of whether or not he was gradually becoming bored by the academic style.

That Renoir could not join his friends in their modern outlook which demanded the glorification of the moment is now understandable. Life and art were for Renoir one and the same thing, nourished from the same source, and if one can compare the other artists to candles which quickly burn out, then one can compare Renoir to a plant which slowly but surely develops, always turning its blossoms toward the sun throughout the long summer, bears rich fruit, and withers. The circle of painters in the Café Guerbois, who had been scattered by the war, met again after the end of the Civil War of 1871 and threw themselves into their work with enthusiasm, unperturbed by the sometimes desperate situation. Renoir had spent the war months comparatively quietly in a regiment in Marseilles. The portraits of a captain, Darras, and his wife may be from this period. They are brilliantly painted, but they lack the atmosphere which one can feel, for example, in the earlier portrait of Sisley. It is true that the contours are still harder there than in the Darras portraits, the colors harder and drier. But that cannot disguise the fact that the spirit of Sisley fills the picture from frame to frame in an indefinable fashion. The background is alive, and there is not merely a model in the clothes, but a personality. *Captain Darras* was painted by Renoir on commission as a show piece with the whole of his technical ability. There was, however, no inner relationship with this man and his world, and so he could not incorporate it in his picture.

Monet, who had fled to England during the war, now took over the leadership of the group again, which, to begin with, was more of an artistic unity than an organized one. In 1872 he had rented a house in Argenteuil near Paris on the banks of the Seine in order to be able to live with his beloved motifs — water, sailing and rowing boats, woods and meadows. Renoir

Orange Seller, 1885-90. Red chalk

THE LUNCHEON OF THE BOATING PARTY, 1881
Oil on canvas, 51″ × 68″ (129.5 × 172.7 cm)
The Phillips Collection, Washington D.C.

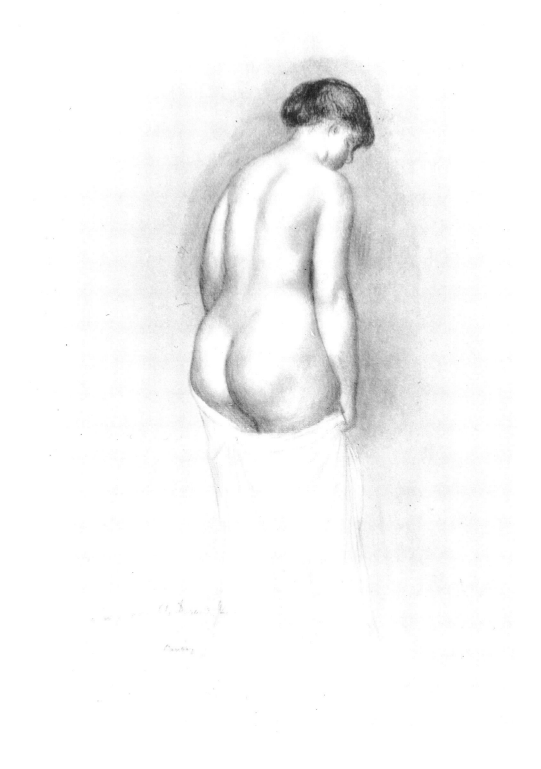

Woman Bathing, 1883. Red chalk

often visited him there at work. They sat next to one another with their easels, and together discovered ways of translating what they saw into light and color. Gradually the figures and things in Renoir's works lost their clumsiness, and the heavy, earthy quality of some of his figures, taken over from Courbet and still traceable in his *Bather* of 1870, began to disappear. Renoir now freed himself from Courbet's influence, and turned to Delacroix as his ideal, but his dependence on his new hero is different, more subtle. Renoir has become surer, his colors are taking on a new independence, making it inevitable that he should turn to Delacroix. It is true that, but for the existence of a few pictures with Oriental motifs, which both in form and content were consciously painted after Delacroix's works, it would be a difficult task to prove this influence simply on the strength of the landscapes and portraits. One would search vainly for Delacroix's wild, glowing colors in, for example, *The Loge* of 1874.[1] Perhaps one could here point out the darkly glowing background, the combination of violet, gold, and black in the foreground, and compare them to Delacroix's Oriental splendor of color, and perhaps one could find something of Delacroix's interiors in the picture *Woman at the Piano*.[2] Here a piece of velvet and some gilded mouldings, there a glittering candleholder on the piano, a colored carpet. In another picture a few especially daring touches of color where the influence of the painter of *Women of Algiers* is evident. The essence of what Renoir found in Delacroix, however, is so thoroughly assimilated that his hero is hardly more than a catalyst which has quickened up the process of development, the awakening of color to a life of its own, to vibration. This process of development also brings with it a loosening up of contours. In accordance with the theory of marginal radiation, which was later to become part of the Impressionist color theory, the contour is abandoned. The physical phenomenon, that two adjacent colors cannot be sharply distinguished from one another by the human eye because their radiation overlaps where they meet to form complementary colors, thus making the margins become undefined, is emphasized in the work of art. A comparison of *Portrait of Sisley* with the later *The Loge* clearly shows the development. The brilliant white of the neckerchief in the portrait is sharply separated from the dark jacket and the somewhat lighter waistcoat. Where are such contours on the couple in *The Loge*? The white shirtfront of the man and his black evening dress form a zone of transition which veils the margins of the two color areas, and on the dress of the young woman black and white flicker, disperse, and merge into one another. Nevertheless they never mix to form a gray, because the brush always places small

Woman at Her Toilet, 1916. Red chalk

(1) See p. 10.
(2) See p. 26.

37

Pencil Study for the Portrait of Julie Manet, 1887. Private collection, Paris

patches next to one another, without having previously mixed them on the palette. That is left to the eye of the spectator.

What Renoir had for the first time done instinctively in the picture painted by the Grenouillère with coarse brush strokes now becomes a principle of composition. He logically reduces the brush strokes to a round comma shape, so that the flickering and vibration now cover the whole picture. This technique, which Monet used for many years, and Pissarro continued to use even right up to his last pictures was finally perfected by Signac with the help of mathematical calculation. For Renoir, it was only a stage of development. He always had command of many possible ways of representing color and light, and used the particular technique that suited his artistic intention of the moment. Thus he was continually finding new ways of representing the world in the medium of color. With a daring which recalls

Head of a Woman. Charcoal drawing

Girl with Basket.   Red chalk

the later Monet he unfolds over the Seine in the Argenteuil picture an atmospheric color display beginning on the left with pinkish gold tones, in which here and there, and more often toward the middle, a blue appears. A dramatic battle between day and twilight takes place above the boats, whose sails — in colors ranging from harsh white to blue — join in. And the whole is intensified by the reflection in the water.[1] During the same period, however, Renoir painted other pictures with a pastellike smoothness which recalls his training as a craftsman. A delicate glaze lies on the face of the woman in *The Loge.* The fleeting pink of the cheeks changes in soft transitional tones to the ivory glow of nose and forehead, with the sharply defined mouth below. Only the eyes are given soft contours, which lend the gaze a certain dewy quality. A similar mixture of techniques can be found in *Les Grands Boulevards.* Here, however, there are no meticulously painted details. Everything vibrates and flickers in that mild light of Paris so fascinating to painters. The moistness of the air lends the colors a special intensity, never making them harsh and loud, however, for the softly blue sky mutes them to a mat glow. This blue sky is painted very thickly in Renoir's picture compared to the green of the trees. *Les Grands Boulevards!* — that is a landscape after Renoir's own heart. An exciting feast for the intellect and the senses. A moist breath of air drifts across from the Seine, and mixes with the dust of the streets and the scent and tobacco smoke of the parading

(1) See p. 5.

Dance in Town
1883
Oil on canvas
71″ × 36″
(130 × 90 cm)
Musée du Louvre
Jeu de Paume, Paris

DANCE AT BOUGIVAL
1883
Oil on canvas
71⅝″ × 38⅝″
(181.8 × 98.1 cm)
Museum of Fine Arts
Boston, Massachusetts
Anna Mitchell
Richards Fund

ladies and gentlemen. Here and there the sound of a laugh, a child's voice, rises above the surging crowds, against the background sound of horses' hooves and elegant carriages.

The decade between the end of the war in 1871 and the year 1882, when the Impressionists exhibited for the last time as a group in the Exposition des Indépendants, was for Renoir a time of development from careful searching to an obvious nec plus ultra of volatilization of form and activation of color via increasing control of the means of expression, and even their occasional routine application. During this decade Renoir and his friends lived in close intellectual and social community with a group of revolutionary artists whose central figure was Manet. Manet, though by no means an Impressionist in the strict sense, dominated by his personality. His sparkling charm and the brilliance of his argumentation, combined with a somewhat dandyish snobbishness, which he consciously cultivated to maintain the distance between himself and his inferiors, predestined him to be the leader, or, to put it more accurately, spokesman of the group. Manet had given up his haunt, the Café Bade, before the war, and now frequented the Café Guerbois, which still exists today on the Avenue de Clichy as Brasserie Muller. In the evening discussions—and what else could the painters do after dusk except meet for discussion, since in the age of petroleum lamps it was not possible to work after nightfall—in these discussions the themes were painting in the open air, the admission to exhibitions, the importance or lack of importance of the old masters for contemporary art, cultural politics, the great importance of Delacroix, and the debatable position of Courbet. One can imagine the fervor of these discussions, in which men of such different temperament and intellect took part. There were Manet and Degas, the one witty, the other caustic, Pissarro, a moderate socialist and convinced atheist with the courage of his principles, but also a man of great kindness and always ready to help others. A rare guest was Cézanne; noncommittal, taciturn, he expressed his opinions with vehemence and could not bear to be contradicted. Apart from the painters Braquemond, Fantin-Latour, Guillemet, Constantin Guys, Monet, and Sisley, the writers Duranty, Zola, and Duret, and the photographer Nadar were frequently present. It was in Nadar's studio on the Boulevard des Capucines that the first memorable Impressionist exhibition took place in 1874.

Many descriptions of the people and happenings of this decisive decade were provided by the authors of contemporary letters and documents. There are also interesting descriptions of Renoir who, when he was not visiting his friend Monet in Argenteuil, or his parents in Louveciennes, or, toward the end of the seventies his friend and patron Bérard on his estate in Normandy, was a frequent guest at the Café Guerbois. Like many of his friends he had never had the opportunity for an education such as Manet or Degas had had, and it was therefore difficult for him to join in the discussion with watertight arguments. Apart from that it was difficult for him, a thoroughly untheoretical person, to see why, for example, Zola was so annoyed by the nymphs in Corot's woodland pictures, and wanted to see peasant women in their place. It was sufficient for him if they were well painted. Renoir, slim, mobile, and modest, was, despite his poverty, of an irresistible gaiety. He was unashamed of his Parisian dialect, and was prepared to laugh at any joke, even if it was not as intellectual as those of Degas. For him life was full of joy and beauty, and he was daily enchanted with it. He could not understand why one should worry oneself with serious theoretical

THE DAUGHTERS OF CATULLE MENDÈS, 1888. Oil on canvas, 64⅛″ × 51¼″ (163 × 130 cm)
Collection Mr. Walter H. Annenberg, New York

discussions about the past, present, or future. This optimism of his was severely tested again and again. He had to fight against the indifference or disregard of the public, the brusque refusal from the official institutions, and an often bitter poverty. But he was not alone in this battle. However much his comrades may have differed in their ideas, they were united in their determination to open up new paths for painting whatever the opposition. Out of this desire was born the idea of arranging, at their own expense, an exhibition which should include for the first time works by artists who were pursuing new artistic aims. Thus, on April 15, 1874, an exhibition of pictures by Cézanne, Renoir, Degas, Guillaumin, Monet, Berthe Morisot, Pissarro, and Sisley, was opened at Nadar's, the photographer's, studio. Among other works, Renoir exhibited *The Loge* and *Dances.* It was an ironic touch of fate that this very exhibition should have given a name to the whole movement. Monet exhibited a picture which he had painted in Le Havre, called *Impression, Rising Sun.* The critic Louis Leroy picked out the first word for the title of his article in «Charivari,» *Exposition des Impressionnistes,* and thus the group was named. The venture turned out to be a scandal as well as a commercial failure. Renoir came in for less calumny than the others owing to his tamer pictures. The rage of the public was vented mainly on Cézanne and Monet. Phrases like «ludicrous collection of absurdities» and «painters who have declared war on beauty» were used in the reviews, and the story went round that the Impressionists painted by filling a pistol with paint and then shooting blindly at the canvas. There is a touch of tragi-comedy about the fact that hardly a hundred years later, a certain section of the public, though surrounding itself with reproductions of Impressionist works, and smiling disdainfully at the ignorance of the public of that time, was using similar foolish comparisons about its own contemporary painting.

Discouraged from further communal undertakings by the failure of both this exhibition and the auction at the Hôtel Drouot in the following year, Renoir tried hard to secure more portrait commissions. The stubborn idealism of a Monet or Cézanne was foreign to him. He was prepared to compromise and paint the kind of works that his clients wanted. A story Ambroise Vollard had from Renoir illustrates this point: «And the trouble I had to get the money, whenever I did by chance get a paid commission! I can remember the time, for example, when I painted a portrait of a bootmaker's wife, for a pair of boots. Every time I thought I had finished and began to think hopefully of my boots, an aunt, or daughter, or even a housemaid, would come in: "Don't you think that my niece, my mother, the Mistress, has a much shorter nose than that?" I wanted my boots, and gave the shoemaker's wife a nose like Madame de Pompadour's.»

During the years 1874-75 Renoir was given strong moral and financial support by the art dealer Durand-Ruel, who, with courage and a sure instinct, gambled on the Impressionists by buying their pictures for a long period without at first being able to sell any at all, by Caillebotte, a well-to-do amateur and ship's engineer, who painted for pleasure and bought pictures—mainly those unsaleable pictures of his friends, and by Chocquet, a civil servant who spent his not very large income on works by Cézanne and Renoir. In 1876 this circle of patrons and friends was joined by Charpentier, the publisher of the journal «La Vie Moderne,» and later by the diplomat Paul Bérard. Among other things, Renoir

Washerwoman and Studies for a Portrait, 1890-95. Red chalk. Private collection

LADY WITH WHITE HAT, 1895. Oil on canvas, 25⅝″ × 21¼″ (65 × 54 cm)
Private collection, Tokyo

Hat Trimmed with Flowers, 1897. Lithograph

received from all of them countless portrait commissions which saved him from the extremes of poverty. Many of the portraits from this period are still painted with great caution. One can sense the trouble that the painter took to achieve physical resemblance. Despite this, the portraits of the young Rivière, an avant-garde writer,[1] and Chocquet, the white-haired art-lover and collector,[2] are extremely lively. Intelligence, sparkling esprit, and nervous sensibility play about the mouth and eyes of Choquet; his hand is touching his chin, but only, it seems, for a moment, then it will break into restless movement again. The muted colors, blue-white and greenish tones dominating, give the picture a certain solemnity. But above all one senses a fascinating discrepancy between this man with his eloquent eyes and the impersonal, conventional background. The brush technique in the *Portrait of Georges Rivière*, carried out in restless small commas and strokes, is much livelier. The intellectual courage, recklessness, and excitability of the young writer are reflected in every form and every color. Conventional taste also plays a part here in the way the head is turned into profile position, which, in a certain sense, reduces the physiognomy to a symbol, and in the green background. Again the personality of the sitter seems to rebel against the severity of the form. Such a refined form of painting, with its most subtle spiritual values as can be found in these two pictures, particularly in that of Chocquet, can, however, no longer be described. The 18th century, with its unique art of portraiture, manifested brilliantly in the miniatures alone, is behind this picture. There have been, perhaps, more powerful portraits, those of Dürer, El Greco, Rembrandt, and Goya, for example, where the person represented casts a spell over the spectator, crushes him with the strength of his personality, overwhelms, or fascinates. But there can scarcely be another portrait painted with so little pretentiousness as that of Chocquet, whose goodness, intelligence, and urbanity touch us afresh every time we look at it.

Jeanne Samary, too, a young, very beautiful Parisian actress, who was a frequent visitor to Renoir's roomy studio in the Rue St. Georges, sat for two pictures, a full-length and a half-length portrait.[3] Now the final step to a thorough-going Impressionist technique is taken in the portrait,[4] as it has already been taken in landscape. The unmixed colors are applied thickly, blue and green in small strokes and points, irregularly placed on the décolleté dress; a couple of dabs of color represent the stones in the gold bracelet. In the upper half of the picture the colors seem to be moving, the red of the background creating the impression of a boiling liquid, on the right darker scraps are drawn into the vortex. This movement has also taken possession of the coppery gold hair. Individual strands flicker outward from the center like the protuberances of a fiery star, surrounding the face with an aura. Toward the middle the forms and colors consolidate. The red of the mouth and the blue of the eyes are like a crystallization of the turmoil of colors surrounding them. The color structure also calls for musical comparisons. One is reminded of theme and variations, of Wagner's «Leitmotive.» Indeed, such comparisons have a certain validity, for Renoir was deeply interested in music. Charles Gounod, Renoir's music teacher, was the first to awaken the boy's interest, and this interest was kept alive in later life by his friendship with the musician Chabrier, and with

(1) See p. 13.
(2) See p. 28.
(3) See p. 29.
(4) Museum of Occidental Art in Moscow.

Faure, the baritone of the Paris Opera, and finally by his enthusiasm for Wagner's music, which was acclaimed by the Impressionists mainly for the way it broke with traditional forms. Here, too, as in the Chocquet portrait, the personality is given a façade in keeping with conventionalism. The pose and the full-face position with its uninhibited, coquettish gaze, attributes of the actress, and a certain importunity of the colors, belong to the theatrical world.

In these works Renoir takes his first steps in the dangerous career of the fashionable portraitist. The commissions secured for him by his patrons and friends poured in. Renoir was in vogue. The publisher Charpentier, who commissioned portraits of his wife and children from Renoir, introduced him, who had so far but rarely ventured into socially higher circles than that of the small circle of his painter friends, to the world of the intellectuals in Paris. Zola, Edmond de Goncourt, Flaubert, Daudet, Maupassant, and Turgeniev were regular guests in Madame Charpentier's salon. It was inevitable that the sensitive painter should now also capture this mondain world in his pictures. A typical example of this is the family portrait *Madame Charpentier and Her Children*.[1] The effect, with the formal pose of the woman and the two small girls in the luxurious salon, is very conventional and fashionable. The wonderful sheen of the silky materials, and the charming faces of the children, however, give the picture the same artistic quality as distinguishes the portraits of Samary, which always lends his pictures a quality of timelessness. The only really Impressionist feature of this family portrait is the still life in the background: the table set with flowers, fruit, and glasses in front of the red wallpaper and the colorful curtain. Only here was Renoir's artistic temperament given full rein, and, just as if he was once more invoking Delacroix, he succeeded in combining splendor with sparkling color, as a contrast to the smooth beauty of the painted materials in the foreground.

As he expected, this family portrait and the portrait of Samary ensured his acceptance into the Salon of 1879, if perhaps more by reason of the famous subjects than of their artistic qualities. But still, he did receive 1,000 francs for the family portrait—a princely sum, if one considers the fact that many painters in those days had to be content if they could get a hundred francs for a picture.

Ever since the first Impressionist Exhibition in Boulevard des Capucines and the unsuccessful auction at Drouot's, the Impressionists had had to fight hard against the indifference of the public and violent attacks in the press in order to maintain not only their artistic, but also their material existence. It was a battle of life and death in the truest sense of the word. Sisley died in utter poverty and despair, and Monet attempted to commit suicide. In their extreme distress the painters formed into a close community. They helped one another selflessly by introducing each other to art dealers and collectors. In 1873 Renoir was introduced by his friends to Durand-Ruel, who immediately bought a few of his pictures, and through Degas he met Duret, one of the few art critics who had already unconditionally declared for the Impressionists. In Argenteuil Monet had made friends with Caillebotte, the owner of the neighboring estate, and immediately introduced Renoir to him. Soon Caillebotte included Renoir in his friendship, and bought his pictures also. Renoir, for his

(1) See pp. 22-23.

part, had hardly been given a commission by Chocquet, when he took him to Père Tanguy's paint shop, to show him Cézanne's pictures. Cézanne then took Chocquet to Monet's studio. It is known that even Manet hung his friends' pictures in his own studio when he was expecting a visit by a well-to-do collector. On the other hand there were bitter fights within the group concerning who should be invited to take part in the Impressionist Exhibition and who should not. In 1877, for the third Exhibition of the group, all the Impressionists were represented together for the last time: Cézanne, Renoir, Degas, Monet, Morisot, Pissarro, Sisley. But from then on the group gradually disintegrated. Renoir began to be given recognition by the Salon. After 1877, he took part only once more in the Impressionist Exhibitions, in 1882. But by that time he no longer really belonged to the Impressionist Group. He had given up painting in the open air and his journey to Italy in the previous year had prepared the way for a new phase in his work.

The five years before that, however, had brought forth the first great harvest. One may have followed with a certain impatience Renoir's cautious approach to the Impressionist technique in the beginning. Already his *Lise* raised hopes that the liberation of color was imminent, and these hopes were fulfilled in a few pictures, among them the *Regatta at Argenteuil.* At the same time, however, his development appeared to be slowed down in the series of impressive portraits, which to a certain extent represented his «official» production. It was only after the year 1876 that all the works which we count among the masterpieces of Impressionism were produced: *The Swing,* [1] *Le Moulin de la Galette* (1877), *The First Evening Out,* [2] *The Luncheon of the Boating Party.* [3] It is possible to select a whole series of masterpieces from Renoir's works without including a landscape — something that would be impossible with any of the other Impressionists — for Renoir's optical susceptibility is directly dependent on people, or, more precisely, on women and girls, and the feminine element becomes stronger and stronger in his later works. The two friends on the bench in *Le Moulin de la Galette* are not only the formal, but also the spiritual centre of the picture. And if one glances from there toward the dancing couples, one's eyes come to rest on the young girl in the left foreground, gracefully leaning against her partner. Bright laughter seems to mix with the sound of music drifting across the scene, and the warm sunlight, casting bright patches on the gay company, lending radiance to the Sunday dresses of the women, their hair, and their faces. The people created by Renoir are always filled with a warm joy of being. This emotion forms a part of the tense expectancy of the young girl in the picture *The First Evening Out,* and of the playful flirtatiousness of the company of rowers in *The Luncheon of the Boating Party.*

The Fêtes Champêtres of the 18th century, with their dances, swings, and picnics are recreated here in a different guise; less refined, more bourgeois, more robust, but full of urgency, and, through the feast of color, heightened to feasts of life. «Cancelled Feasts» was what Meier-Graefe called Renoir's phase of development between 1881 and the turn of the century, a very apt term which justly characterizes what was happening in Renoir's painting at that

(1) See p. 9.
(2) See p. 11.
(3) See pp. 34-35.

Women Bathing, 1884-85. Red chalk. Private collection, Paris

54

THE BATHERS, 1887
Oil on canvas
46³⁄₈″ × 67¹⁄₄″
(117 × 171 cm)
Philadelphia Museum of Art
Collection of Mr. and Mrs.
Caroll S. Tyson

Girl at Her Toilet. Red chalk

time. His contemporaries also had the same feeling about it — they were disappointed that the splendid series of sensual and colorful Impressionistic feasts, from *Lise*, *Le Moulin de la Galette*, *Jeanne Samary*, to *The Luncheon of the Boating Party*, had come to an end. Ingres became Renoir's new ideal. It was just as if, after a ballet, the warm, colorful lights of the performance were suddenly replaced by the cold lights of the auditorium, and the spectators did not hesitate to show their disappointment. The circle of Renoir enthusiasts was horrified, his rich patrons turned away from him, and the Impressionists, for whom Ingres was on the same level as Antichrist, treated him as a deserter.

In *Thérèse Bérard*,[1] painted in 1879, one can already sense a cooling off despite all the magic of the delicate glaze on the face and clothes, a cooling off, however, which increases the psychological depth of the portrait, and which, as one may well predicate on the grounds of several other group portraits of the Bérard family, is even completely consistent with the spirit and character of the sitter. Here we are again reminded of a painting on enamel. Delicate transitional tones link the softly luminous areas, and the compact silhouette in front of a neutral background classifies the work as a conventional portrait. The *Lady with Veil*,[2] too, differs, as far as color is concerned, from the works of previous years. The delicate pastel shades hardly recall the past at all, and the plane composition of the picture, the conspicuous emptiness of the right half, point rather to Japanese influence, which indeed was rife everywhere after the World's Fair in Paris in 1867, with its Oriental pavilions. Bracquemond, Whistler, and Degas collected Japanese art and Oriental jewellery and many of their works show Eastern influences, and Toulouse-Lautrec's posters of the nineties are unthinkable without Utamaro and Hokusai. Renoir himself did not like the subtle color harmonies of the Japanese woodcuts, but that does not exclude the possibility that in his new uncertainty he borrowed his pastel shades from the Japanese. It would be quite wrong to fix the date of the beginning of the crisis as early

Woman with Child

(1) See p. 15.
(2) See p. 14.

Coco Painting, c. 1906.   Red chalk

as this. If we had not the visual evidence of his pictures of the following twenty years, we should probably have no misgivings, but the break did not come, in fact, before 1883, and was then much more radical. What, however, is evident from the pictures of the years 1879 and 1880, is a basic change in Renoir's relationship to Impressionism.

This change came after a journey to Italy, during which he visited Venice, Rome, Naples, and Florence. While in Venice, he had absorbed and utilized the magic of Southern color, the colorfulness of that city on the lagoon and its iridescent atmosphere. During his stays in Rome, Naples, and Florence he only visited the museums, enthused about Raphael, and discovered the Pompeian frescoes for himself. In his pictures from Venice, *Gondola on the Canale Grande* and *San Marco, Venice*,[1] he once more pulled out all the stops. The surface shimmers with glorious color, the brush seems to have been riotously flurried across the canvas, to transform the town into a fantastic mirage. That was the last feast, exuberant, intoxicated, and already somewhat unreal. We no longer participate with all our senses as we did in *The Luncheon of the Boating Party*, where our eyes could pleasurably flirt with each patch of color. Here colored veils have interposed. The curtain is about to fall.

From Venice Renoir went on to Rome and studied Raphael's frescoes. Their beauty made a deep impression on him. The old conflict of line versus color, which Renoir, working with his friends, had decided in favor of color ten years before, began in him anew, and he prepared himself to take on the heritage of Ingres, the great French master of the line: The heritage which, with the Impressionists, he had up to now denied. Now he was able to draw upon earlier experiences, his discovery, for example, of one of Ingres' pictures, the portrait of a woman which hung in the Louvre next to the *Jewish Wedding* by Delacroix, which he was copying. Even at that time he sensed the clarity of the composition and the beauty of the line. Ingres remained his secret, unavowed love, until it finally became apparent under the influence of the Raphael frescoes. The question of why this change took place calls for an answer. The artist gave an answer to this question to Vollard, who recorded it in his biography of Renoir, as follows: «I had followed Impressionism to the utmost limits, and was forced to come to the conclusion that I could neither paint nor draw. I had reached a

(1) See p. 31.

58

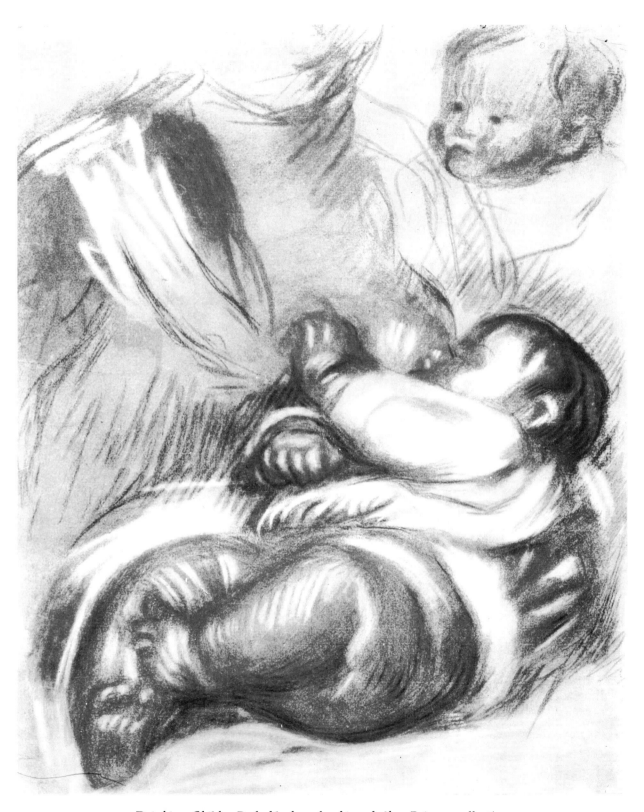

Drinking Child. Red, black and white chalk. Private collection

Woman Drying Herself. Pen and ink drawing. Musée du Louvre, Paris

BATHER ON A ROCK, 1892. Oil on canvas, 31½″ × 25⅛″ (80 × 64 cm)
Private collection, Paris

RECLINING NUDE, c. 1890
Oil on canvas, 13″ × 16″ (33.5 × 41 cm)
The Norton Simon Foundation, Pasadena, California

▷

SLEEPING BATHER, 1897
Oil on canvas, 32″ × 25″ (81 × 65.5 cm)
Collection Oskar Reinhart « Am Römerholz, » Winterthur, Switzerland

63

WOMAN PLAYING THE GUITAR, 1897. Oil on canvas, 39″ × 31″ (81 × 65 cm)
Musée des Beaux-Arts, Lyons, France

dead end.» Perhaps this is the first place in Renoir's development where the word genius may be applied without reservation. Remembering the late works of Pissarro and Monet in which the «limits of Impressionism» are sometimes painfully obvious, one is deeply impressed by the power of genius which was able to guide the artist through difficult years of struggle and search, to new pastures. Here, too, there are crescendoes and climaxes, but there is always a slow but steady overall growth.

Thus there is no real break to be seen even after the Italian journey. With the impression of Raphael's work fresh on his mind he painted while he was still in Italy a *Blonde Bather* whose gleaming, voluptuous body has the summarily painted sea as background. Here he naively combines Ingres and Raphael and creates a being in whom the «joie de vivre» of the south is coupled with the coolness of the north. But that is presumably the only nude that he painted on the journey. Having

Ambroise Vollard, 1904. Lithograph

returned to the South of France, he spent February 1882 recuperating from the violence of the Italian light, in L'Estaque, where he met Cézanne, and a few landscapes were produced in the mild climate of the Côte d'Azur. *L'Estaque* is an example. Here Renoir draws upon his experiences of the seventies: blue-violet shadows on the ground in the wood, bright touches of sun in the green-blue grass. Cézanne appears to have had no influence on Renoir's landscape painting at the time. There is none of the tectonic severity, none of the articulation in small rectangular patches of color, already used by Cézanne at that time in the composition of his pictures. A charming coastal landscape, perhaps a little overcolorful on the whole, spreads itself out behind the framework of trees and branches in the foreground: effective Mediterranean magic. One would be much more justified in discovering Cézanne's sponsorship in the still life with the *Fruits from the Midi*.[1] This picture is not a piece of colorful, atmospheric gossamer, but a well-composed collection of twenty-four different fruits, clearly distinguished from one another by their drawing and color. And the color already has something of the dryness of Cézanne's pictures, and appears to have been applied with rough brushstrokes. The picture is dated 1881, however, that is, earlier than the meeting. But this question is, after all, unimportant, compared with the fact that here the form is consolidating and the colors are being used again more objectively, and this might just as

(1) See p. 72.

well have been brought about by the impressions gathered in the museums in Italy as by the influences of a contemporary's painting.

Renoir brought another very important asset back with him from Italy: Enthusiasm for fresco. How weary he must have been of Impressionism, for his eyes were capable of being opened to the beauty of Raphael's frescoes and the grandness of his composition. The first results of his experiences in Rome were a few pictures in large format from the year 1883, in which he takes up again the beloved Impressionist motif of dancing in the open air, but now completely brought into line with his new conception. *Dance at Bougival*[1]: Here we again have the coffee-garden under shady trees, as in *Moulin de la Galette*, the young snub-nosed thing at the table, chatting with the beaux from *The Luncheon of the Boating Party*. In front of the lightly painted background, however, is the statuesque figure of Suzanne Valadon, a very popular model of that day, pupil of Degas and later independent painter, and mother of Utrillo. Next to her, her dancing partner, for whom Edmond, Renoir's brother, was the model. This work already incorporates some mural elements. The background, despite all the Impressionist speckledness, is so muted in color that the dancing couple, painted in large areas and with strong contours, takes on great prominence. The aim at a decorative effect, with the pyramidal structure rising from the great width below up to the dancer's yellow hat, should, however, not be mistaken. The girl, clinging to her rough partner in the waltz, is one of the most delightful of Renoir's creations, and one feels that the painter not only found it easy, but positively enjoyed painting her in such a large format. In a single stream of movement the lines sweep up from the swinging skirt to the red scarf which in turn leads to the chin, from where the movement opens into the roundness of the face. The man is much stiffer and clumsier, the contours are unwieldy, and the dark blue of the jacket and trousers is dead and dry. It is significant that these first symptoms of crisis in Renoir's painting should appear in the male figure, but not yet in the female, whose grace and charm still so fascinated the painter that he was once again able to overcome all his artistic scruples and uncertainty. And if there was anything that was also later constantly to save Renoir from the crisis, it was the natural magical quality that he could sense in women and children.

With *Dance in Town*,[2] although it was painted in the same year, we have already reached the dry period. The luminous quality has gone from the colors, the volatile, colored veils of his earlier pictures seem to have been driven off by a gust of cold air, and the forms are sharply distinguished from one another as in the rarefied air of high mountains. The colors are almost academically smooth, although there is a charming duet for blue and green. Mural ideas have a stronger effect in this picture, and the economical coloring of the large areas is again influenced by Japanese colored woodcuts. This Eastern art, however, did not have a lasting influence on Renoir. He only made use of it while he was in search of new creative principles. His hero remained Ingres, whose influence, as *The Umbrellas*[3] shows, had awakened Renoir's interest in the formal qualities of things, and their plastic

(1) See p. 43.
(2) See p. 42.
(3) See p. 16.

Louis Valtat, c. 1904.   Lithograph

representation in a three-dimensional setting. The comical shape of the umbrellas, with the formal discord provided by the bent ribs and rounded surfaces on the one hand, and the pointedness and sharp ridges of the edges on the other hand, proved such an attraction for Renoir that he based the composition of the picture on it. The spectator's gaze is directed into the background, and upward through a lane of swaying domes. It then follows the upright figures downward, only to rise again. Renoir successfully attempted to transfer the centre of gravity into the upper quarter, and thus, as it were, to «hang» the picture from that point. A reversal of the normal principle of composition, which places the basis of the picture in the lower half. It is still a completely moot point whether Renoir arrived at this unusual solution by experimenting with such abstract principles of composition, or whether the idea was simply suggested to him by the particular shape of the umbrellas. In the following year, however, he began work on a picture whose complicated composition is the result of countless sketches, both of details and of the composition as a whole: *The Bathers*[1] — the artistic and stylistic climax of the dry period. The picture has an almost programmatic character. The Impressionist technique, which is still used for the two children in the right foreground in the picture *Umbrellas*, plays nothing more than a very minor role in the landscape in the background of *The Bathers*. The wonderful harmony of movement of the four figures, however, is reminiscent of Classicist reliefs, and the many intersections of the legs of the two sitting women are so balanced that they give the impression of belonging rather to a choreographic study than to a gay bathing party. With a wonderful open gesture one of the women draws space into the picture, and at the same time focuses the group into the foreground. The very natural pose of the woman standing up to her waist in the water, lifting up her hair with both hands, allows the picture to fade out toward the background on a weaker accent. The plastic shaping of the bodies, never stiff, never sculptural, is achieved by the mother-of-pearl luster given to the skin, which, even in the shadowed parts and in the creases, never shows a trace of gray, preserving even there a delicate, lively luminescence. The picture may betray the fact that Renoir took great pains over it, that the composition and both the application and combination of colors were the result of much experiment — but it is nevertheless completely free of tedium and pedantry. This work, on which Renoir probably spent three years, was the fulfilment of the promise inherent in *Dance in Town* — the consolidation of form and line into a monumental gesture.

In his choice of theme, and even in some of the details of posture, Renoir was inspired by a relief by Girardon in the Gardens of Versailles, a fact to which Meier-Graefe drew attention. This point is actually of less importance for the understanding of this picture, than for the whole of Renoir's development. The mere realization that Renoir discovered Ingres' art while still emulating his antithesis Delacroix, reduces the chasm between the Impressionist and dry periods. Still more does the fact that in turning to an earlier, antiquating ideal he once again found contact with his past Impressionist period, during which, after all, he had frequently taken the compositions of the great masters as his inspiration. Florisoone[2]

(1) See pp. 54-55.
(2) *Renoir*, Hypérion, Paris, 1938.

STILL LIFE WITH PEACHES AND GRAPES, 1881. Oil on canvas, 21″ × 25½″ (53.3 × 64.7 cm)
The Metropolitan Museum of Art, New York. Mr. and Mrs. Henry Ittleson Jr. Fund

ANTIBES, 1893
Oil on canvas, 25⁵⁄₈″ × 31⁷⁄₈″ (65 × 81 cm)
Private collection, London

◁

Dancing Girl with Tambourine
Study

FRUITS FROM THE MIDI, 1881. Oil on canvas, 20″ × 25⅝″ (50.8 × 65 cm)
The Art Institute of Chicago. Collection Mr. and Mrs. Martin A. Ryerson

devotes a whole chapter to Renoir's relationship to tradition, pointing to, among other things, the relationship of some of his pictures with pictures by Rubens, Titian, and Vermeer, and of course to Watteau's *Embarkation to Cythera* and Boucher's *Diana in the Bath*, which Renoir had admired even as a boy. This positive attitude toward tradition is completely consistent with his remark, recorded by Vollard: « I was only myself when I could study in a museum.» Even if it should not be taken literally, it is nevertheless no less than a reverent recognition of the artistry of the Old Masters, who, unaffected by short-lived modern styles, always remained a timeless and valuable example for him. This recognition also includes, in Renoir's case, the painting technique, which had once been thrown overboard in the general abandonment of tradition by the Impressionists. Because of his training and his experience in porcelain painting, Renoir, in contrast to his friends, felt that he owed something to traditional craftsmanship. For him, the durability of the canvas, its expert priming, the neat application of paint, and careful experimenting to discover the percentage of oil most suitable for a paint, were an essential part of the quality of a picture. Albert André[1] collected remarks of Renoir's concerning his art, and they show that he was an artist who thought very conscientiously about problems of craftsmanship. One of these remarks was: « I prefer a kind of painting which is fat and oily, and as smooth as possible. That is why I love oils so much. In order to achieve the results I have always desired, I have tried every kind of technique... I have tried painting with dots, in order to obtain better transitions from one tone to the other; but this technique results in a rough surface, and I don't like that very much...» When a picture « is painted with this pointillist technique, I am always tempted to strike my matches on it. Apart from that, dust settles in the interstices and changes the tone values. A picture should be able to survive all varnishes, all dirt, and all the maltreatment which time and restorers can bring.»

This attitude of Renoir's toward the work of art — so foreign to the Impressionists — is also based on his study of Cennini's « Tract on Painting,» which he came across in 1883, and which he studied particularly with regard to the technique of fresco painting and the old paint recipes. This purely theoretical knowledge was aptly supplemented by his studies in Italy, where he studied the technique of the frescoes of the 15th century. Renoir now approaches his work very carefully, he paints out, scrapes the paint off, and begins again. He frequently makes new sketches and traces them on to the canvas. He never thought much of the Impressionist conviction that the genuine work of art could only come into being by a lightninglike reproduction of the first impression. But now he becomes overcareful and even uncertain, so that it is actually only at this time, that is, after the painting of *The Bathers*, that one can really speak of a crisis. The transition from the domination of color to the domination of the line had taken place painlessly and without hiatus, whereas he found the return to color in the late eighties and the nineties hard. Often he lacked the courage to put a single dab of color on the canvas, and even felt it necessary to go to the neighboring studio of a fashionable painter for advice. One is shocked by the shrill, poster-like red and green of *La Coiffure* of 1888. Parts of the canvas might almost have been painted by a housepainter,

(1) *Renoir*, Crès, Paris, 1919.

The Artist's Son Jean, 1900. Oil on canvas, 21¾″ × 18¼″ (55.2 × 46.4 cm)
The Art Institute of Chicago. Collection Mr. and Mrs. Martin A. Ryerson

PORTRAIT OF COCO, c. 1900   Oil on canvas, 12¼″ × 10⅛″ (30 × 25 cm)   Private collection

and the delicate pink of the seated girl's dress, its pink delightful nuance which so often appears in his later works, where it adorns voluptuous female bodies, here has an unpleasant obtrusiveness. Despite all the transformation of form and color, however, the female body retains its natural grace even here. The somewhat coquettish turn of the head which does not try to evade the carefully working hands, but nevertheless wants to be seen to its advantage—«en face»—was caught by the eye of a painter who could not be distracted from nature however engaged he was by problems of form and theory of art. Nevertheless there are pictures which lack even these qualities, and in which the uncertainty is as shockingly obvious as it is in the family portrait of 1896 (Barnes Collection, Merion, Pa.) with the painter's wife, his two sons Jean and Pierre, the nanny, Gabrielle, and a girl from the neighborhood. The colors are dull, the forms are doughy rather than soft. Sometimes it seems as if the contours cannot contain the heavy masses of color, which spread and become bloated. The figures stand stiffly and clumsily next to one another, and the composition lacks all spontaneity. For the first time the people in Renoir's pictures are posing. Even if they had done so in previous years he had always been able to give them a natural composure and charm in the work of art. This creative power seems to have failed him in some of the works he painted before the turn of the century. It would be unfair to the artist to conceal these undeniable temporary lapses. To do that would be to belittle the severity of the battle which he had to fight, and detract from the greatness of his victory over the crisis. Now and then there are happy moments when a work like *Bather on a Rock* [1] of 1892 was produced. The skin may no longer have the delicate freshness of the early Impressionist nudes, nor the enamellike glaze of the eighties, but light plays a creative part in the shaping of the body, it has penetrated it and illuminates the breast and arms from within, giving it the appearance of Parian marble under a Greek sky. The wonderful, artlessly coquettish gesture of the left hand, too, makes up for much that is unnatural and artificial in these years, and shows that feminine beauty can still make the painter forget all his scruples and open the way to naively great creations.

One of these great creations was a meadow landscape with two young girls in the foreground, painted between 1890 and 1894. With this picture Renoir had already taken a decisive step away from his linear style, had opened form to color again, and had apparently returned to Impressionism. But only apparently, for the invaluable gains of the past years were by no means relinquished. The approximately fifteen years older picture *Lady with Parasol*, [2] from Renoir's Impressionist period, with a similar motif, makes an enlightening comparison. In a comparison of this kind we are not interested in differences in quality, but in the fact that light and color have a different meaning in each picture. In the earlier work the light comes from an outside source, the sun, and despite all the freedom that Renoir allows himself in the use of broad brushstrokes, the illuminated and shadowed parts are quite distinct from one another—the large splashes of sun in the grass, and the play of

(1) See p. 61.
(2) See p. 25.

The Post-Office House at Cagnes, 1906. Oil on canvas, 18⅛″ × 21⅝″ (46 × 55 cm)
Private collection, Tokyo

STILL LIFE WITH FLOWERS, 1890
Oil on canvas, 25⁷⁄₈″ × 32¹⁄₈″ (65.7 × 81.6 cm)
The Metropolitan Museum of Art, New York. Gift of Raymonde Paul

ROSES IN FRONT OF A BLUE CURTAIN, 1908
Oil on canvas, 19″ × 21″ (48 × 54.5 cm)
Private collection, Paris

light and shadow on the woman's dress. Strong contrasts are achieved by the use of tones ranging from white to a dark, almost black, green, and yet, how much poorer in light is this picture than the landscape with the two girls: Here it is unnecessary for an outside source of light to illuminate the scenery and bring the colors to life, for even the darkest green in the trees and the reddish brown of the hair is still as bright as if the paint were luminescent. Renoir also no longer needs the light-dark effects for the composition of a picture. On the basis of his experience during the Ingres period he gives the picture a simple and firm structure: The upright trunks of the sitting girls and the groups of trees on both sides are rhythmically balanced against one another. The prominent figure in the foreground, which takes up a great deal of space, balances the cluster of trees on the right, whereas the half-hidden bright figure of the girl in profile formally corresponds to the delicate tree on the left of the picture. There is none of the fortuitousness, the brusque overlappings, the highlights of the Impressionists, but none of the smoothness and austerity of form, and none of the uncertainty of the coloring of the period of crisis either. The structure of the picture is retained, but it no longer gives the impression of being dependent on a penciled outline. It is simply there, without any conscious thought. It is the result of a self-imposed hard asceticism, during which Renoir renounced color to gain mastery of form. Soon afterward there was the dangerous period in which the newly acquired force of form got out of control, when he tried to fill it with color again. Finally he overcame the weakness, but only with the aid of his beloved motifs: women bathing, women against a country background, or with children. The secret of this development can hardly be grasped rationally—it is as though a memory of happy times, which had been overshadowed by hard, bitter years, had now been recaptured slowly under the influence of a simple melody from his youth. Thus there are scarcely any pictures of children by Renoir, even from the period of crisis, in which he does not effortlessly succeed in reproducing their apple-cheeked freshness and delicacy. Renoir covered many yards of canvas with the faces of children and young girls—there are countless portraits just of his sons Pierre and Jean, and later especially of Coco, whom he painted at every imaginable occupation.[1] These motifs accompany Renoir throughout his life. There are often several of them, lightly sketched, in one picture. It is as if he sought recreation in these gentle exercises from the strain of his great compositions. Flower and fruit still lifes play a similar role. They make one forget all the past wrestling with theoretical problems. Red, in all its many nuances, surges across the pictures, mixes with green and white to form a wild maelstrom of color which seems about to swirl out of the frame. A song of praise to nature, her riches, beauty, and fertility. And these three things remain Renoir's main themes until the day of his death.

Renoir's outward life developed particularly successfully from 1886-1900, the very years of his artistic crisis. Nearly every winter he was able to spend a few months in the South of France. He hated the winter, and painted only one winter picture. He once called snow

(1) See pp. 74 and 75.

« nature's scab. »   In the summer he returned to Paris with his wife and children and the nanny Gabrielle.   There are countless pictures of Gabrielle, who was his model for many years: after bathing, combing her hair, with his children, in country clothes, reading.[1] The picture *Gabrielle with the Rose* in the Louvre shows her coarse beauty.   Here he has hung a blouse loosely around her, whom he had so often represented in the nude, in order to contrast the luster of her skin with the dull white of the material.   Once Renoir had found a model whose skin satisfied his artistic ideals, he did not like to part with her again. Thus Gabrielle stayed for many years in his household.   The brother of the collector Caillebotte, who was a frequent guest of Renoir's, once said after a dinner: « Extraordinary, I never get a fish soup at home like the one I get at the Renoirs'...   And yet I have a proper cook...   The only thing that is expected of a cook at Renoir's is that she should have a skin that looks well in the light...»

Now Renoir also had considerable success with the public, especially as a result of his exhibition at Durand-Ruel's in 1892.   In the same year he was even able to record his first sale of a picture to the State.   When, however, in 1894, as executor of his dead friend Caillebotte, he offered Caillebotte's collection of Impressionist paintings to the State, he was to meet with only reluctant, and partial acceptance.   And that collection included masterpieces by Degas, Manet, and Cézanne.   Henri Roujon, the then Director of the Académie, accepted only a few pictures by Degas and Manet, and only one of Renoir's, *Moulin de la Galette.* He rejected Cézanne completely.   However, Renoir no longer needed to worry about the recognition of his own art, especially after his second successful exhibition at Durand-Ruel's in 1896.   He was 55 years old, could look back on great achievements, and could feel the power and passion to strive for new goals ever increasing within him.   He lived happily in the circle of his family.   Now that he was assured of financial security by the regular sale of his works, he was able to buy a house near Essoyes not far from Paris.

There he suddenly suffered a heavy attack of rheumatism in 1898, but was able to fight it off by taking the waters at Aix-les-Bains.   In the following years, however, his illness became worse, traveling became painful, and he was finally confined to an invalid's chair.   The illness, no doubt a kind of rheumatoid arthritis, affected his whole body, he grew thin and his face became emaciated.   Finally fate delivered him a last, terrible blow, in that the disease crippled his hands.   This misfortune affected both the man and the artist equally — and both emerged from the trial with superhuman greatness.   Vollard records how Renoir, during the time when his illness was already very advanced, considered himself lucky, and overcame the difficulties and pain with a humor that put everybody else to shame.   The man mastered his life with humor, the artist — with his art.

His works become more and more self-assured, one might almost say classical.   *The Church at Cagnes* of 1905: green, yellow ochre, and blue, and a few vertical lines which offset the

(1) See pp. 85 and 88.

PORTRAIT OF MADAME RENOIR, 1910. Oil on canvas, 32″ × 25⅝″ (81.3 × 65 cm)
The Wadsworth Atheneum, Hartford, Connecticut. Collection Ella Gallup Summer and Mary Catlin Collection

Self-Portrait, 1914. Pencil

oblique lines of the roof, are the components of the picture. There is no longer any complicated directing of the gaze. From left and right the eye is led to the front of the church and then upward, following the giant cypresses. The people in the church square have apparently been only summarily painted in, and yet the few dabs of color suffice to characterize every single person even by his clothes. Renoir also achieved classical greatness in his still lifes, which, however, were never cool or austere. One only has to look at the few strokes of the brush which sufficed for the underside of the saucer in *Still Life with Cup* (1905) and compare this with *Fruits from the Midi* of 1881, which then suddenly appear rather ostentatious. The underside of the saucer's edge alone has more artistic qualities than all the colorful fruits together. The surface of the table is reflected, and so is the green of the plant on the right, and only an occasional gleam of the porcelain's own color, blue and white, shows through. Everything is simpler, quieter, and at the same time richer. It is a deeply moving experience if, when looking at Renoir's late pictures, one suddenly recalls the fact that at the time when he transferred these paradisiacal visions on to canvas he was already suffering so much from his illness that he could no longer grasp the brush properly, but had to slide it between his crippled fingers. Two self-portraits from the year 1910 show the physically broken man with his wasted face—overwhelming confessions of a man tortured by all the pains of age, but unwaveringly working on and remaining true to his vocation throughout agonizing days and years until the end.

It was in this badly handicapped condition that he painted his most mature works in Cagnes, where he lived toward the end of his life on his small estate Les Collettes. Once again it becomes clear how smoothly his creative development progressed. It is as though the genius of his art had postponed this trial until it was incapable of damming his creative powers. It came at a time when he no longer needed direct contact with nature. Saturated with everything which his eyes could absorb, he had long since considered painting in the open air unnecessary, even troublesome, because the direct sunlight affected too strongly the degrees of brightness on palette and canvas. Pure landscape had gradually disappeared from his painting, and he now almost entirely restricted himself to representing the nude female body. He never painted without a model—that he had learned from Diaz—but he scarcely looked at her any longer. The visions appeared before his inner eye, and found their way onto the canvas.

The works of the last ten years, up to his peaceful death on December 3, 1919, at the age of seventy-eight, are completely devoid of weight, they are no longer earthbound. They seem to be visions from another, sun-bright world: Playful, nude girls in a rural setting, or on the banks of a river, and *Bathers* in endless variety. His palette, which, after the « dry » period with its cobalt blue and its earthy colors, had at first appeared to become richer—it then included madder lake, cinnabar, brownish red, yellow ochre, Naples yellow, chrome green, green earth, cobalt blue, ivory, black, and white—is now limited to a few colors only—cinnabar, ochre, Naples yellow, black, and some white. With these colors, however,

GABRIELLE WITH JEAN RENOIR AND A LITTLE GIRL, 1895
Oil on canvas, 25⅝" × 31⅞" (65 × 81 cm)
Private Collection, U.S.A. Courtesy Acquavella Galleries, Inc., New York

he created works which no longer prompt the question of how they were «made,» or pose problems of technique and style. One recognizes these pictures, in which contours of people and surroundings are blurred and everything is joined in a concord of color, as manifestations of a pantheistic philosophy. It is after all completely unimportant that a picture from 1913 should be called *The Washerwomen*. Fort it is after all not the occupations—the washing, rinsing, and wringing—however explicity they may be described, which fascinated the painter, but the colorful, lively scene on both sides of the stream. Here we once more have the Rococo pastoral scene as an iconographic basis. With only a slight alteration of the attributes we should have here a gay open-air party. A bathing party by the water, on the left bank two women dancing, in the right foreground a mother with her child, picnicking. And even the stone caryatid, invariably to be found in the background of an 18th century «fête galante» is here, in the shape of a washerwoman, balancing her basket on her head with nonchalant grace. If the joy of living is heightened here by an occupation, by movement, in other pictures it is deepened by the feeling of stillness, by the consonance with nature in which the figures find themselves: *Two Women with a Young Girl in a Landscape*. This consonance is not the resul of a romantic, prodigal abandonment of oneself to nature as to something different and alien. These female figures have their roots in the soil, are themselves nature, and have the natural beauty of everything that grows. The nude female figures in Renoir's late pictures, also, whether they are in a forest setting, by lakes or rivers, like the *Bathers*,[1] or in a room, have this same naturalness. They are not undressed, for these natural bodies appear never to have known clothes. Their nudity is their natural clothing, as the fur is to the animal or the bark to the tree. Even there, where the erotic element might be present—in the partly exposed, voluptuous shoulder and neck of the *Woman Tying Her Shoe*,[2] one of Renoir's last works—it is nevertheless just as remote as it would be in a landscape. But his women and girls are, however, always blooming, lively creatures, possessing all the beauties of this world. It is true, though, that they do not enjoy life's pleasures on this earth, but in the lustrous regions of a paradisiacal innocence—or, in plain words, in the paintings of Renoir.

Renoir worked hard throughout his life, and now that he was confined to an invalid's chair he worked harder than ever. He had been thrifty with time in order to be able to create the great number of his masterpieces. He even at one time, when he was given hope of curing his illness, refused to do so for the sake of his art. Vollard tells of Renoir's meeting with the famous doctor, Henri Gautiez: «As a result of Doctor Gautiez' treatment Renoir succeeded in taking a few steps without assistance. And when the doctor told him that with daily exercises and by the utmost concentration of his will-power... "But", interrupted the painter, "and my painting?"—And Renoir sat down in his chair once more, never to leave it again.»

(1) See p. 92.
(2) See p. 89.

Mother and Child, 1902. Pencil

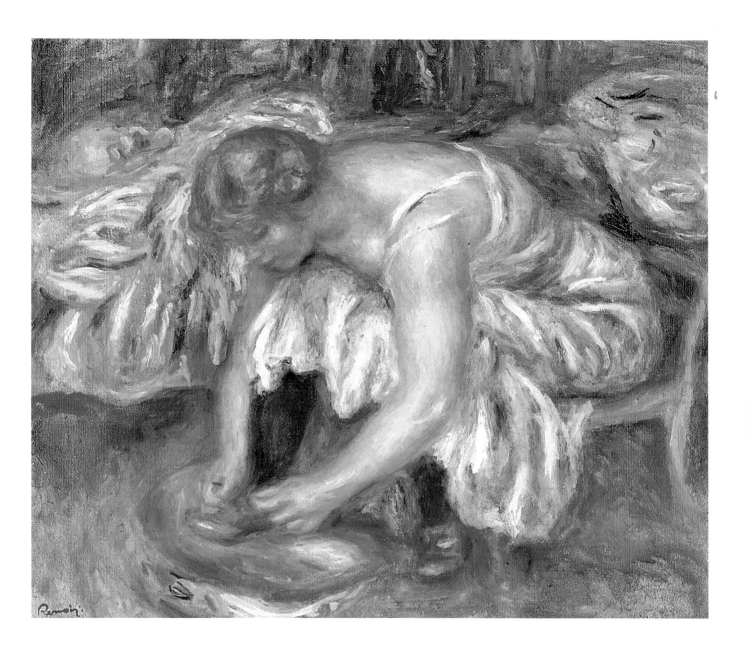

◁
GABRIELLE WITH BARE BREASTS, 1907
Oil on canvas, 22″ × 18″ (56 × 46 cm)
Private collection, France

WOMAN TYING HER SHOE, c. 1918
Oil on canvas, 19⅞″ × 22¼″ (50.5 × 56.5 cm)
Courtauld Institute Galleries, London. The Courtauld Collection

BIOGRAPHY

1841 Born in Limoges on February 25, the son of a tailor.

1845 His family moves to Paris (Rue d'Argenteuil).

1849 Attends the neighborhood school, where Charles Gounod, the composer, awakens his interest in music.

1854 Is apprenticed in a porcelain factory, where he decorates ceramics in the eighteenth century style. Later he also decorates fans and screens.

1862 Attends classes at the Ecole des Beaux-Arts in Paris. He also frequents Gleyre's studio, where he meets Sisley, Bazille, and Monet. Pissarro and Cézanne, both attending the Académie Suisse, become his friends.

1863 Leaves Gleyre's studio. Studies at the Louvre with Fantin-Latour.

1864 Meets Diaz while painting in the forest of Fontainebleau. *La Esmeralda*, a picture painted in academic style, and later destroyed by Renoir, is accepted by the Salon.

1865 Paints with Sisley in Marlotte. Two pictures at the Salon.

1866 Paints *Le Cabaret de la Mère Anthony* in Marlotte. Rejected by the Salon in spite of Corot's and Daubigny's support. In the spring, paints with Monet in Paris. Works in Bazille's studio.

1867 *Diana Hunting* rejected by the Salon.

1868 *Lise with Parasol* at the Salon, with favorable reviews. Paints a ceiling in Prince Bibesco's villa.

1869 Paints with Monet in Bougival, on the same themes: Views of the boathouse La Grenouillère, bathers and boating parties. With his model Lise at Ville d'Avray.

1870 *Bather* and *Algerian Woman* at the Salon, with favorable reviews. Called up to serve in the 10th Regiment of Cavalrymen at Bordeaux.

1871 Portraits of Captain Darras and his wife, Returns to Paris during the Civil War of 1870-71. Painting trips to Louvecienne and Bougival.

1872 Studio in Rue Notre-Dame-des-Champs. Visits Monet in Argenteuil. Views of Paris (*Quai Malaquai, Pont-Neuf*). Introduced to Théodore Duret by Degas.

1873 Meets Paul Durand-Ruel, who becomes his dealer. Large studio in Rue Saint-Georges.

1874 Seven paintings at the Impressionist Exhibition at Nadar's studio. Friendship with Caillebotte, a collector and a painter. *The Loge*.

1875 Unsuccessful auction at the Hôtel Drouot (pictures by Renoir, Monet, Sisley, and Berthe Morisot). Meets Chocquet, a collector.

1876 Fifteen pictures at the Second Impressionist Exhibition. Studio in Rue Cortot, in Montmartre. Paints *The Swing* and *The Moulin de la Galette*. Friendship with the publisher Georges Charpentier, the Daudet family, and the actress Jeanne Samary.

1877 Twenty-two pictures at the Third Impressionist Exhibition. *Portrait of Jeanne Samary*.

1878 Stay at Pourville, near Dieppe. Paints *Madame Charpentier and Her Children*.

1879 *Madame Charpentier* is exhibited at the Salon, to great critical acclaim. In June, one-man show at the gallery « La Vie Moderne. » First stay with the diplomat Paul Bérard and his family at their seaside home in Wargemont on the Channel, near Dieppe. Drawings for the magazine « La Vie Moderne. »

1880 Growing doubts about his own paintings. Starts *The Luncheon of the Boating Party*. Studio in the Rue Norvins. Summer at Berneval.

1881 Journeys to countries where the sunlight is intense: Algeria, Italy, and the south of France. Falls under the influence of Renaissance painters, especially Raphael, visits the museums of Rome and Florence, discovers Venice, is deeply impressed by the frescoes at Pompeii.

1882 *Portrait of Richard Wagner* in Palermo. Twenty-five pictures at the Seventh Impressionist Exhibition.

1883 With Monet in Marseilles and Genoa. Visits Cézanne in L'Estaque. Paints *Dance at Bougival* (model Suzanne Valadon) during a stay in Guernsey.

1884 Paints in Paris and in La Rochelle. Ceases to be a strict Impressionist.

1885 Birth of his son Pierre. Sketches for the large *Bathers*. Stay at Wargemont and, with Cézanne, at La Roche-Guyon.

1886 Impressionist Exhibition organized by Durand-Ruel in New York. Exhibition of the XX in Brussels. International Exhibition at the Georges Petit Gallery in Paris.

1888 Stay with Cézanne at Jas-de-Bouffan; spends winter in Martigues.

1889 At Cézanne's in Montbriand, near Aix-en-Provence.

1890 Studio in Boulevard de Clichy. Exhibits for the last time at the Salon. Visits Berthe Morisot in Mézy.

1891 Short trip to Spain.

1892 First sale of a painting to the French State. Trip to Spain with Gallimard. Stay at Pont-Aven (Brittany). Murals for Durand-Ruel. Philippe Gangnat buys his first Renoir pictures.

1893 Birth of his son Jean. Winter at Beaulieu (Provence), summer at Pont-Aven. His children's nanny, Gabrielle, becomes his favorite model.

1894 Death of Caillebotte, who bequeaths his collection to the State. Renoir is made executor. Studio in Rue Tourlaque.

1895 Travels to Provence, to Holland and to London.

1896 Exhibition at the Durand-Ruel Gallery. Trip to Bayreuth.

1897 Through Renoir's efforts the Caillebotte bequest is accepted for the French national collection (including six paintings by Renoir). Stay at Berneval.

1898 Buys a summer house at Essoyes in the Champagne province, the birthplace of his wife.

1899 First bout of arthritis compels him to spend the winter in the south of France.

1900 Stays in Grasse, Saint-Laurent-les-Bains, and Louveciennes. Awarded the Legion of Honor.

1901 Birth of his son Claude (Coco). Takes the waters at Aix-les-Bains.

1902 Settles in the south of France, at Le Cannet.

1903 Winter at Le Cannet, summer at Essoyes. *The Garden* at Essoyes. Rents « Les Collettes » near Cagnes.

1904 Takes waters at Bourbonne-les-Bains for his arthritis. The Autumn Salon is a triumph for him.

1905-09 Worsening rheumatism. *The Judgment of Paris* (1908).

1910 His health improves and he can travel to Munich.

1912 Badly crippled with arthritis. Made Officer of the Legion of Honor.

1913 Major exhibition at the Bernheim-Jeune Gallery in Paris.

1914 Outbreak of war. Pierre and Jean are wounded. Death of his wife.

1919 Visit to the Louvre after a summer at Essoyes. Dies on December 3, at Cagnes.

BATHERS, 1910. Oil on canvas, 15¾″ × 20″ (40 × 51 cm)
Nationalmuseum, Stockholm

BIBLIOGRAPHY

ANDRÉ, Albert. *Renoir*. Paris: Georges Besson, 1918. Crès, 1919, 1928.

ANDRÉ, Albert and ELDER, Marc. *L'Atelier de Renoir.* 2 vol. Paris: Bernheim-Jeune, 1931.

BARNES, Albert C. *The Art in Painting.* Merion, Pa: The Barnes Foundation Press, 1925.

BARNES, Albert and DE MAZIA, Violette. *Art of Renoir.* New York: Milton, Bach & Co., 1935.

BASLER, Adolphe. *Pierre Auguste Renoir.* Paris: Gallimard, 1928.

BEAUDOT, Jeanne. *Renoir, ses amis, ses modèles.* Paris: Editions littéraires de France, 1949.

BESSON, Georges. *Auguste Renoir.* Paris, 1929.

BLUNDEN, M. and C. *Journal de l'Impressionnisme.* Geneva, 1970.

BORGMEYER, C. L. *The Masters Impressionists.* Chicago, 1913.

BÜNEMANN, Hermann. *Renoir.* Ettal: Buch-Kunstverlag, 1959.

CABANNE, Pierre and al. *Renoir.* Paris, 1970.

CALLEN, Anthea. *Renoir.* London; Oresko Books, 1978.

CATINAT, Maurice. *Les Bords de la Seine avec Renoir et Maupassant.* Chatou: Editions S.O.S.P., 1952.

CATTANEO, Irene. *Vita colorata di Renoir.* Milan: Bietti, 1947.

CLAY, Jean. *L'Impressionnisme.* Paris: Hachette, 1970.

COGNIAT, Raymond. *The Impressionists.* New York, London: Hyperion, 1951.

COGNIAT, Raymond. *The Century of the Impressionists.* New York: Crown, 1967.

COQUIOT, Gustave. *Renoir.* Paris: Albin Michel, 1925.

CORTISSOZ, Royal. *Personalities in Art.* London: Scribner, 1925.

CORTISSOZ, Royal. *The Painter's Craft.* London: Scribner, 1930.

DAULTE, François. *Frédéric Bazille et son temps.* Geneva: Pierre Cailler, 1952.

DAULTE, François. *Watercolors, pastels and drawings in color.* Trans. by Robert Allen. New York: Abrams. London: Faber & Faber, 1959.

DAULTE, François. *Renoir, catalogue complet de son œuvre.* 4 vol. Paris, Lausanne: Durand-Ruel, 1971-1975.

DAULTE, François. *Auguste Renoir.* Milan: Fratelli Fabbri, 1972.

DRÜCKER, Michel. *Renoir.* Paris: Tisné, 1944, 1949, 1955.

DURET, Théodore. *Manet and the French Impressionists.* London: Richards, 1910. Philadelphia: Lippincott, 1912.

DURET, Théodore. *Renoir.* New York, 1937.

FEZZI, Elda. *L'Opera completa di Renoir nel periodo impressionista, 1869-1883.* Milan: Rizzoli, 1981.

FEIST, P. H. *Auguste Renoir.* Leipzig: Seemann, 1961.

FLORISOONE, Michel. *Renoir.* Paris, London: Hyperion. 1937.

FOSCA, François. *Renoir.* Trans. by Mary J. Martin. Englewood Cliffs, N. J: Prentice Hall, 1961.

FROST, Rosamund. *Pierre Auguste Renoir.* New York: Hyperion with Duell, Sloan & Pierce, 1944.

GAUNT, W. *Pierre Auguste Renoir.* London, 1953.

GAUTHIER, Maximilien. *Renoir.* Paris: Flammarion, 1976.

GRABER, Hans, ed. *Impressionisten Briefe.* Basel: Schwabe, 1934.

GRABER, Hans. *Auguste Renoir nach eigenen und fremden Zeugnissen.* Basel: Schwabe, 1943.

HAESEAERTS, Paul. *Renoir, sculptor.* New York: Reynal & Hitchcock, 1947.

HOPPE, Ragnar. *Städer och konstnärer; resebrev och essäer om konst.* Stockholm: Bonniers, 1931.

LASSAIGNE, Jacques. *L'Impressionnisme.* Lausanne, 1966.

LETHÈVE, J. *Impressionnistes et symbolistes devant la presse.* Paris, 1959.

LEYMARIE, Jean. *Renoir.* Paris: Hazan, 1949.

LHOTE, André. *Peintures de Renoir*. Paris: Le Chêne, 1944.

MEIER-GRAEFE, Julius. *Impressionisten*. Munich, Leipzig: Piper, 1907.

MEIER-GRAEFE, Julius. *Renoir*. Munich: Piper, 1911. Leipzig: Klinkhardt & Biermann, 1929. Paris, 1912.

MEIER-GRAEFE, Julius and HAUSENSTEIN, W. *Renoir*. Munich, 1920, 1929.

MIRBEAU, Octave. *Renoir*. Paris, 1913.

MONNERET, Sophie. *L'Impressionnisme et son époque*. 4 vol. Paris, 1978-1980.

NEMITZ, Fritz. *Auguste Renoir*. Cologne: Phaidon, 1952.

PACH, Walter. *Pierre Auguste Renoir*. New York: Harry Abrams, 1950.

PERRUCHOT, Henri. *La Vie de Renoir*. Paris: Hachette, 1964.

RAYNAL, M. *Renoir*. Geneva: Skira, 1949.

RENOIR, Jean. *Renoir, my father*. Trans. by Randolph and Dorothy Weaver. Boston: Little Brown, 1962.

REWALD, John. *History of Impressionism*. 4th rev. ed. New York: Museum of Modern Art, 1980.

RIVIÈRE, Georges. *Renoir et ses amis*. Paris: Floury, 1921.

ROBIDA, Michel. *Renoir : Children*. Trans. by Diana Imber. New York: French and European Publications, 1962.

ROGER-MARX, Claude. *Renoir*. Paris: Floury, 1933.

ROGER-MARX, Claude. *Les Impressionnistes*. Paris: Hachette, 1956.

ROUART, Denis. *Renoir*. Geneva: Skira, 1954.

SALMON, André. *Propos d'atelier*. Paris: Nouvelle Edition Excelsior, 1938.

SCHNEIDER, Bruno. *Renoir*. Berlin: Safari Verlag, 1957.

SCHNEIDER, Bruno. *Renoir*. New York: Crown, n.d.

TERRASSE, Charles. *Cinquante portraits de Renoir*. Paris: Floury, 1941.

THYIS, J. *Renoir den franska kvinnans mälare*. Stockholm, 1944.

VENTURI, Lionello. *Archives de l'Impressionnisme*. Paris: Durand-Ruel, 1939.

VINDING, Ole. *Renoir*. Stockholm: P. A. Norstedt, 1951.

VOLLARD, Ambroise. *Tableaux, pastels et dessins de Pierre Auguste Renoir*. 2 vol. Paris: Ambroise Vollard, 1918. 2nd ed. Paris: Alain C. Mazo, 1954.

VOLLARD, Ambroise. *Renoir, an intimate record*. Trans. by Harold Van Doren and Randolph Weaver. New York: Knopf, 1925.

VOLLARD, Ambroise. *Ecoutant Cézanne, Degas, Renoir*. Paris: Grasset, 1938.

WILDENSTEIN, Daniel. *Renoir*. Paris: Vergennes, 1980.

WILENSKI, Reginald H. *Modern French Painters*. New York: Reynal & Hitchcock, 1940.

EXHIBITIONS

University of Miami, Coral Gables, Fla. *Renoir to Picasso, 1914*. Feb.-March 1963.

Musée Cantini, Marseilles. *Renoir peintre et sculpteur*. June-Sept. 1963.

Galerie Knoedler, Paris. *Renoir*. June-Sept. 1966.

Galerie Durand-Ruel, Paris. *Renoir intime*. Jan.-Feb. 1969.

Wildenstein Galleries, New York. *Renoir*. March-May 1969.

Musée de Troyes. *Renoir et ses amis*. June-Sept. 1969.

Salon d'automne, Paris. Auguste Renoir. Oct.-Nov. 1970.

Seibu Galleries, Tokyo. Cultural Centre, Fukuoka. Museum of Modern Art of the Hyogo District, Kobe. *Renoir*. Oct. 1971-Feb. 1972.

Art Institute, Chicago. *Renoir*. Feb.-April 1973.

Wildenstein Galleries. *Renoir, the Gentle Rebel*. Oct.-Nov. 1974.

Hotel Bristol, Paris. *Renoir*. Nov. 1974.

Museum of Arts, Fort Lauderdale, Fla. *The Graphic Work of Renoir from the collection of Dr. Stella*. 1982.

LIST OF ILLUSTRATIONS

We wish to thank the owners of the pictures reproduced herein, as well as those collectors who did not want to have their names mentioned. Our special thanks go to Mr. François Daulte in Lausanne for his kind and valuable assistance:

MUSEUMS

FRANCE

Musée des Beaux-Arts, Lyons – Comédie Française, Paris – Musée du Louvre, Jeu de Paume, Paris.

SWEDEN

Nationalmuseum, Stockholm.

UNITED KINGDOM

Courtauld Institute Galleries, London – The National Gallery, London.

UNITED STATES OF AMERICA

Boston, Museum of Fine Arts – Cambridge, Massachusetts, The Fogg Art Museum – Chicago, The Art Institute – Cleveland, Museum of Art – Hartford, Connecticut, The Wadsworth Atheneum – Minneapolis, The Institute of Arts – New York, The Metropolitan Museum of Art – Philadelphia, The Museum of Art – Portland, Oregon, Art Museum – Richmond, Virginia, Museum of Fine Arts – Washington D.C., National Gallery of Art; The Phillips Collection – Williamstown, Massachusetts, Sterling and Francine Clark Art Institute.

PRIVATE COLLECTIONS

Walter H. Annenberg, New York – Norton Simon Art Foundation, Pasadena, California – Oskar Reinhart Collection « Am Römerholz, » Winterthur, Switzerland.

GALLERIES

New York, Acquavella Galleries Inc.

PHOTOGRAPHS

E. Irving Blomstrann, New Britain, Connecticut – Jean Loup Charmet, Paris – A. E. Dolinski, San Gabriel, California – Bernard Lontin, La Tour de Salvagny (Lyons) – Studio Lourmel, Paris – Service de Documentation Photographique de la Réunion des Musées Nationaux, Paris.